Spider Fingerless Gloves

Knit Flat on 2 Needles

by

Janis Frank

Page 2

Thank you for purchasing this ebook. This book remains the copyrighted property of the author, and may not be redistributed to others for commercial or non-commercial purposes. If you enjoyed this book, please encourage your friends to purchase their own copy from Amazon or their favourite book retailer.

Thank you for your support and respecting the hard work of this author. The purchase of this ebook allows you to make and sell the physical items you create.

Copyright 2023 by Janis Frank

All rights reserved.

Table of Contents

Wrong Stitch Counts...........................Page 7

Things You Need................................Page 8

Sizing & Gauge..................................Page 8

The Pattern

      Left...Page 11

      Right.......................................Page 16

Finishing..Page 20

Abbreviations......................................Page 21

QR Code to All Videos.......................Page 23

Help Support My Work......................Page 24

More FREE Knitting Patterns............Page 25

Follow Me on Social Media...............Page 29

Creepy? No. Awesome? YES! Knit a pair of fingerless gloves with a spider motif on the back of the hand. Guaranteed to never fall off, the 3D spider is created as you make the mitten.

A couple words of advice before we get started, this isn't a pattern for beginners. I recommend that you have some basic knowledge of knitting. I also suggest making a pair of my plain **Super Simple Fingerless Gloves** first if you've never made a pair of gloves or mittens before. Thumb gussets can be tricky and there's no point adding in a spider to confuse things even more.

Take a pic of this QR code to read the Super Simple Fingerless Glove pattern online

You'll need to think out of the box a bit for this one; making bobbles and working selectively over given stitches to create the body and head. But the basic glove portion is the same as every other glove with a thumb increase you've made.

This pattern has been in the works for a number of years now. It originally started as a knit in the round design, but because of the extensive purling, there were always lines left where the needles met. I couldn't live with that.

So, there was a change in plans from the initial design. First change; it's knit flat on 2 straight needles. The second is that instead of including a bunch of how-to pictures, and there were going to be a lot, I decided it was time to utilize QR codes. Everything that may be challenging, particularly rows 25 – 27 can be a little confusing. I made videos that show the trickier parts of these rows. To watch the video, take a picture of the QR code with your phone or tablet and the video will pop up. You can watch the video instantly as many times as you need.

If you need help with any of the stitches such as PM1, M1, C1F or C1B there are QR codes in the abbreviation section that will take you to the video demonstrating how to do them.

Wrong Stitch Counts

It is very easy to have the wrong number of stitches created around the spider. This can happen between the gusset for the thumb and the spider, or for the shorter side. If that happens you can take it apart. The other option is to just go with it. Being a stitch or two off won't be noticeable to the wearer.

If you decide to "just go for it", line up the stitches done to create the spider to previous spider stitches. In general, this is just the legs. They are very obvious. Keep in mind that you always knit the legs on the right side and purl the legs on the wrong side. Adjust the background of the mitt with your incorrect count of purl stitches on the right side and the knit stitches on the wrong side.

For example, if you're making Row 30, instead of K7 at the start of the row you made a mistake and now have K8. Knit the 8 stitches instead and start the rest of the pattern from there.

Example row:
    Row 30: K7 *P1 K1* Repeat from * to * 2 *more* times. P1 K6 M1 K11 M1 K12

Things You Need

Worsted weight yarn – a standard ball of yarn (215 yards/197 m)

Knitting needles – described below in sizing and gauge

Cable Needle

Stitch Holder

Tapestry needle to sew the seam and work in the ends

Sizing and Gauge

Like my other fingerless gloves I've designed such as my owl fingerless gloves, I use the size of the needles to change the size of the mitt. This keeps the proportion of the spider consistent to the size of the glove.

My standard for sizing was my hand and designed the knitting pattern according to what kind of rubber gloves fit me comfortably. I wear a medium sized rubber glove and the medium sized glove fits perfectly. You may need to use different sized needles to get the correct gauge, but this pattern is very forgiving if you're a bit off. Most knitting is tbh.

Small - 7.5 cm (2.95 ")

Medium - 8.5 cm (3.35")

Large - 10 cm (3.94")

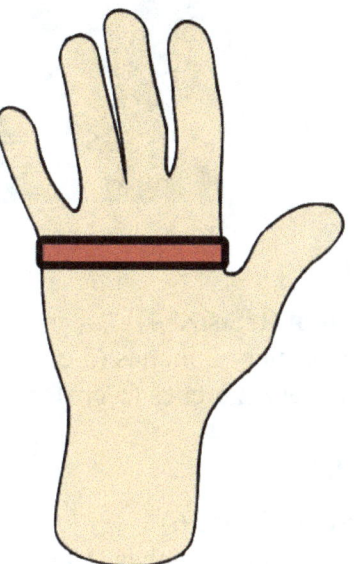

Hand sizing made easy

Small

size 3.5 mm (US size 4)
11 stitches every 2 inches (5 cm)
16 rows every 2 inches (5 cm)

Medium

size 4 mm (US size 6)
10 stitches every 2 inches (5 cm)
14 rows every 2 inches (5 cm)

Large

size 5 mm (US size 8)
9 stitches every 2 inches (5 cm)
12 rows every 2 inches (5 cm)

Left Hand

Cast on 33, loosely

Row 1: K1 P1 across. K last st.

Row 2: P1 K1 across. P last st.

Repeat rows 1 and 2 for a total of 10 rows.

Row 11: P across

Row 12: K across

Row 13: P across

Row 14: K across

Row 15: P12 PM1 P1 PM1 P7 K1 P3 K1 P8   (35 sts)

Row 16: K8 P1 K3 P1 K22   (35 sts)

Row 17: P20 K1 P1 K1 P3 K1 P1 K1 P6   (35 sts)

Row 18: K6 P1 K1 P1 K3 P1 K1 P1 K5 M1 K3 M1 K12   (37 sts)

Row 19: P22 K1 P1 K1 P3 K1 P1 K1 P6 (37 sts)

Row 20: K6 P1 K1 P1 K3 P1 K1 P1 K22 (37 sts)

Row 21: P12 PM1 P5 PM1 P5 C1F twice, P1, C1B twice, P6 (39 sts)

Row 22: K6 *K1 P1* Repeat from *to * 3 *more* times, K25 (39 sts)

Row 23: P25 C1F K1 P1 K1 C1B P7 (39 sts)

Row 24: K8 P2 K1 P2 K7 M1 K7 M1 K12 (41 sts)

Row 25: P28 K2tog, Bobble 6 (K6 into one stitch by alternating knitting into the front and back of the stitch, turn. *** Working the following rows into the 6 stitches in the one stitch***, P6, turn, K6, turn,  P6, turn, K6, turn, P6, turn, K6, turn, P6, turn, K2tog 3 times (do ***NOT*** turn). Pass the middle stitch over the stitch closest to the tip of the needle. Two bobble stitches remain. Pass the second bobble stitch over the stitch closest to the tip of the needle. (The bobble is now 1 stitch again on your needle.) K2tog. P8 (39 sts)

Row 26: K8 PM1 P3tog PM1 K28   (39 sts)

Row 27: P12 PM1 P9 PM1 P7 FB2 (This is a simple increase knit-wise in the next stitch. These are the start of the front legs). Bobble 5 (K5 into one stitch by alternating knitting into the front and back of the stitch, turn. *Working the following rows into the 5 stitches in the one stitch*, P5, turn, K5, turn, P2tog P1 P2tog, turn, K3 (do *NOT* turn). Pass the middle stitch over the stitch closest to the tip of the needle. Two bobble stitches remain. Pass the second bobble stitch over the stitch closest to the tip of the needle. (The bobble is now 1 stitch again on your needle) FB2 (AKA Increase in the next stitch. Makes the other front legs). P8.   (43 sts)

Row 28: K8 P2 K1 P2 K30   (43 sts)

Row 29: P29 C1B K1 P1 K1 C1F P7   (43 sts)

Row 30: K7 *P1 K1* Repeat from * to * 2 *more* times. P1 K6 M1 K11 M1 K12   (45 sts)

Row 31: P30 C1B twice P1 C1F twice P6   (45 sts)

Row 32: K6 P1 K1 P1 K3 P1 K1 P1 K30   (45 sts)

Row 33: P12. Pass the next 13 stitches to a stitch holder. P7 K1 P3 K1 P8   (32 sts)

Row 34: K8 P1 K3 P1 K19   (32 sts)

Row 35: P across

Row 36: K across

Row 37: P across

Row 38: K across

Row 39 - 42: K1 P1 across

Cast off *loosely*.

Making the Thumb

Pick up the 13 stitches on the stitch holder. Transfer them onto the other needle so you start knitting with the **WRONG** side facing you. If you don't transfer them onto the other needle you'll get a line.

Row 1: K across

Row 2: P across

Row 3: K across

Cast off *loosely*.

Right Hand

Cast on 33, loosely

Row 1: K1 P1 across. K last st.

Row 2: P1 K1 across. P last st.

Repeat rows 1 and 2 for a total of 10 rows.

Row 11: P across

Row 12: K across

Row 13: P across

Row 14: K across

Row 15: P8 K1 P3 K1 P7 PM1 P1 PM1 P12   (35 sts)

Row 16: K22 P1 K3 P1 K8   (35 sts)

Row 17: P6 K1 P1 K1 P3 K1 P1 K1 P20   (35 sts)

Row 18: K12 M1 K3 M1 K5 P1 K1 P1 K3 P1 K1 P1 K6   (37 sts)

Row 19: P6 K1 P1 K1 P3 K1 P1 K1 P22   (37 sts)

Row 20: K22 P1 K1 P1 K3 P1 K1 P1 K6   (37 sts)

Row 21: P6 C1F twice, P1, C1B twice, P5 PM1 P5 PM1 P12   (39 sts)

Row 22: K24 *K1 P1* Repeat from *to * 3 *more* times, K7   (39 sts)

Row 23: P7 C1F K1 P1 K1 C1B P25   (39 sts)

Row 24: K12 M1 K7 M1 K7 P2 K1 P2 K8   (41 sts)

Row 25: P8 K2tog, Bobble 6 (K6 into one stitch by alternating knitting into the front and back of the stitch, turn. *Working the following rows into the 6 stitches in the one stitch*, P6, turn, K6, turn,  P6, turn, K6, turn, P6, turn, K6, turn, P6, turn, K2tog 3 times (do *NOT* turn). Pass the middle stitch over the stitch closest to the tip of the needle. Two bobble stitches remain. Pass the second bobble stitch over the stitch closest to the tip of the needle. (The bobble is now 1 stitch again on your needle.) K2tog. P28   (39 sts)

Row 26: K28 PM1 P3tog PM1 K8   (39 sts)

Row 27: P8 FB2 (This is a simple increase knit-wise in the next stitch. These are the start of the front legs). Bobble 5 (K5 into one stitch by alternating knitting into the front and back of the stitch, turn. *Working the following rows into the 5 stitches in the one stitch*, P5, turn, K5, turn, P2tog P1 P2tog, turn, K3 (do *NOT* turn). Pass the middle stitch over the stitch closest to the tip of the needle. Two bobble stitches remain. Pass the second bobble stitch over the stitch closest to the tip of the needle. (There is now 1 stitch on your needle.) FB2 (AKA Increase in the next stitch. Makes the other front legs). P7 PM1 P9 PM1 P12.   (43 sts)

Row 28: K30 P2 K1 P2 K8   (43 sts)

Row 29: P7 C1B K1 P1 K1 C1F P29   (43 sts)

Row 30: K12 M1 K11 M1 K6 P1 *K1 P1* Repeat from * to * 2 *more* times. K7 (45 sts)

Row 31: P6 C1B twice P1 C1F twice P30   (45 sts)

Row 32: K30 P1 K1 P1 K3 P1 K1 P1 K6   (45 sts)

Row 33: P8 K1 P3 K1 P7 Pass the next 13 stitches to a stitch holder P12   (32 sts)

Row 34: K19 P1 K3 P1 K8   (32 sts)

Row 35: P across

Row 36: K across

Row 37: P across

Row 38: K across

Row 39 - 42: K1 P1 across

Cast off *loosely*.

Making the Thumb

Pick up the 13 stitches on the stitch holder. Transfer them onto the other needle so you start knitting with the ***WRONG*** side facing you. If you don't transfer them onto the other needle you'll get a line.

Row 1: K across

Row 2: P across

Row 3: K across

Cast off *loosely*.

Finishing

I recommend that you finish the body of the spider before sewing the seams along the edge. It's easier to work it when flat. I like to make a figure 8 around the body, to the head, around the head, and back to the start.

To give the spider body and head a more rounded feel, cut a length of yarn about 12" long. Insert your tapestry needle from the wrong side through the front between the head and the body. Pick up stitches around the edge of the body, back to the head. Pull snug until you are happy with the body shape

Pick up stitches around the head back to the body. Pull snug until you're happy with the shape.

Pull the yarn to the back of your work. Tie off.

I like to tack the body at it's base to the glove so it won't flop around and stay in line with the head. Tie off.

No need to work in the ends when finishing the spider body and head. Simply pull the yarn through the body of the spider. Press the body down and cut the yarn. When the body pops back up, the end will be hidden in the body.

Once the spider finishing is complete, sew the seams along the edge and the thumb, working in the ends when finished to avoid lumps from knots.

Abbreviations

K - Knit

P - Purl

st – stitch

sts – stitches

P3tog – Purl 3 stitches together

P2tog – Purl 2 stitches together

K2tog – Knit 2 stitches together

K3tog – Knit 3 stitches together

Page 22

PM1 – Make one (purl wise). Increase one stitch between the stitches. Pick up the yarn between the stitches. Twist it slightly and place it on your non-working needle. Purl the stitch. Take a photo of the QR code to see how.

M1 – Make one (knit wise). Increase one stitch between the stitches. Pick up the yarn between the stitches. Twist it slightly and place it on your non-working needle. Knit the stitch. Take a photo of the QR code to see how.

C1B – Cable 1 back. Pick up next stitch on a cable needle. Pull this stitch to the *BACK* of your work. **Knit** the next stitch. **Purl** the stitch on the cable needle. Take a photo of the QR code to see how.

C1F – Cable 1 forward. Pick up the next stitch on a cable needle. Pull this stitch to the *FRONT* of your work. **Purl** the next stitch. **Knit** the stitch on the cable needle. Take a photo of the QR code to see how.

FB2 – Knit in the front and back of the next stitch. This is also known as an increase one in the next stitch. I'm labeling it as this because it is very easy to make a mistake here and pick up an extra stitch. This way I know I have your attention and made you look ☺ No need to thank me..or complain.

QR Code to All Videos

To make this very simple and to take you over to YouTube directly, here is the playlist of all the videos needed to make these gloves. Take a photo with your phone or tablet to watch them play.

Like all of my patterns you have my permission to sell and/or give away the physical items that you make using this pattern. You are NOT permitted to reprint or duplicate this pattern in any form unless you have obtained my written permission to do so.

If you have any questions, please feel free to leave a comment or send me your questions at kweenbee_crafts@hotmail.ca.

Help Support My Work!

Follow me on TikTok, Instagram, Twitter, Facebook, Pinterest and YouTube. Every follow, subscribe, thumbs up, like, heart and share help increase my popularity on the web and get more viewers to my work. It costs you nothing but helps me sooooo much!

If you would like to help a little more, you can always support me on Patreon or you can make a single time donation at Buy Me a Coffee.

Patreon

Buy Me a Coffee

More FREE knitting patterns on my website

This is the latest list of patterns I have on my website. It is an ever growing list so you might want to take a photo of the QR code below wth your phone or tablet. My website with the list of all my latest patterns will pop up on your smart device.

*Take a photo of this square for
FREE knitting pattens on my website!*

If you would like to access any of the patterns you can easily do a internet search to find them, too. When you are on your favourite search engine like Google, Bing, Yahoo, etc. Enter the term ***Kweenbee*** and the title as it is written below (capitalization isn't important). It will pop up for you in the search results and be super-easy to find.

Page 26

For example, enter it like this:

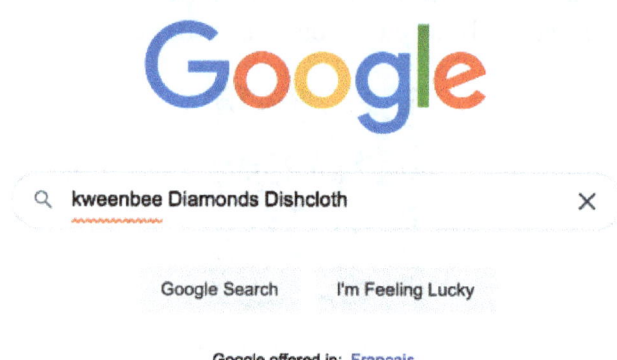

Your results will have my pattern at the very top...usually. Depending on the popularity of the pattern, you may get a link to Pinterest or Ravelry first. Don't worry! All of those options have links back to my original patterns, too!

Winter Beanie Toque or Touque or Tuque with Vertical Stripes

Minimalist Round Toe Slippers – Knit Flat on 2 Needles

One Piece Knitted Dishcloth and Coasters

Knitting for Beginners – Knit a Dishcloth

Easy to Knit Long Cuffed Slippers

Easy to Knit Rolled Cuff Slippers

Knit a Pair of Texting Mitts

Chevron Striped Moccasin Slippers

Super Cozy Textured Adult Bootie Slippers

Textured Easy to Knit Dishcloth Pattern

Super Simple Fingerless Gloves – Knit Flat on 2 Needles

Easy to Knit **OWL** Fingerless Gloves – Knit Flat on 2 Needles

Knit Long Fingerless Gloves – Two Styles with One Pattern

Super Simple Knit Slippers

Cable Fingerless Gloves

How to Knit Fingerless Arm Warmers or Mitts – with Bows!

How to Knit Fingerless Gloves

Bars and Stripes Knitted Dishcloth Pattern

How to Knit Fingerless Gloves – with OWLS!

FREE Knitted Slipper Pattern for Children

FREE Knitted Slipper Pattern for Adults

How to Knit Adult Slippers

How to Knit Ribbed Bootie Slippers for Adults

Adorable Sheep Slippers

Diamonds Dishcloth

Cute AF Bows Dishcloth – FREE Knitting Pattern

How to Knit Slippers Like Granny Made

Knit Two Styles of Slippers with One Pattern

Adult & Child Knitted Slippers…With BOWS!!

Easy to Knit Slippers – Great Beginner Knitting Pattern

Cable Knit Slippers for Children and Adults

How to Knit Socks & Graft a Toe – With Photos

Cable Knit Wine Bottle Cozy or Koozie

Knit a Simple Dishcloth

How to Knit a Way Cool Monster Purse

How to Knit a Cable Scarf aka Netflix and Knit…This Scarf

How to Knit a Pair of Flip Mittens or Fingerless Gloves

How to Knit Adult Bootie Slippers

How to Knit Children's Slippers – Free Knitting Pattern

Knitted Adult Slippers with a Plaid Pattern

Follow Me on Social Media

[Me on Pinterest](http://www.pinterest.com/kweenbee_crafts) - http://www.pinterest.com/kweenbee_crafts

[Like Me on Facebook](https://www.facebook.com/janis.the.knitter/) - https://www.facebook.com/janis.the.knitter/

[Me on YouTube](https://www.youtube.com/user/KweenBeeCrafts) - https://www.youtube.com/user/KweenBeeCrafts

[Instagram](https://www.instagram.com/janis_as_in_joplin) - https://www.instagram.com/janis_as_in_joplin

[Twitter](https://twitter.com/Crafty_Janis) - https://twitter.com/Crafty_Janis

KweenBee.com

[My Etsy Shop](http://www.etsy.com/shop/KweenBee) - http://www.etsy.com/shop/KweenBee

[Become a Patron on Patreon!](https://www.patreon.com/JanisFrank) - https://www.patreon.com/JanisFrank

[Buy Me a Coffee](https://www.buymeacoffee.com/JanisFrank) - https://www.buymeacoffee.com/JanisFrank

Copyright 2023
All rights reserved
Janis Frank

www.ingramcontent.com/pod-product-compliance
Lightning Source LLC
Chambersburg PA
CBHW081130080526
44587CB00021B/3820